בס"ד

(SEFER OTiYOT)

TheBOOKof LETTERS

ספר אותיות

a Mystical Alef-bait

Lawrence Kushner

יעקב בן אברהם קושניר

Jewish Lights
Publishing
Woodstock, Vermont

Sefer OTIYOT: The BOOK of LETTERS.

2014 Hardcover Edition, Eighth Printing
Copyright © 1975 and © 1990 by Lawrence Kushner.

For information address Jewish Lights Publishing, A Division of Long-Hill Partners, Inc., P.O. Box 237, Sunset Farm Offices -- Route 4, Woodstock, VT 05091. Tel: (802) 457-4000, Fax: (802) 457-4004.

First printing, Harper & Row Publishers, Inc., NY, 1975
15th Anniversary 2nd Edition, Jewish Lights Publishing, 1990.

Book & Cover design by Lawrence Kushner
Book produced by Robinson & Kriff

Library of Congress Cataloging-in-Publication Data
Kushner, Lawrence, 1943—
        (Sefer Otiyot)
      ספר אותיות

      In English
      1. Hebrew language -- Alphabet -- Juvenile literature.
I. Title. II. Title: The Book of Letters.
PJ4589.K8   492.4'1'1
ISBN 978-1-879045-00-2
ISBN 978-1-58023-798-7 (eBook)
      10 9 8

Printed in the United States of America.

for Karen

מַעְיַן גַּנִּים
בְּאֵר מַיִם חַיִּים

a fountain of gardens
a well of living waters

Foreword to the 15th Anniversary
Second Edition of
THE BOOK of LETTERS

Fifteen years doesn't sound like a long time -- I mean historically or sociologically or even intellectually. It only seems like a long time when the years have "come out of your life." Both authors and readers can look around & realize that they're not kids any more. Or that their kids have grown up. Or that they've had kids. Or that their kids have become B'nai Mitzvah. Or got married. I look at my own handwriting and realize that I am a different man. Fifteen years ago I could write a legible alphabet, now, I'm up to a few illegible words.

So, in life-time, fifteen years can be a lot of life. Our perspective on what is truly precious in life becomes clarified. And sometimes, often, to our embarrass-ment, things we thought were trivial turn out to be important, and things we were convinced were im-portant turn out to be trivial. So it goes.

I wrote the Book of LETTERS hoping that it might save as a primer to Jewish spiritual awareness. And because I still have that hope, I am happy that it is making its appearance in this second edition. But the real truth is that LETTERS all began as a joke: I inadvertently play-ed on myself.

I had only been out of rabbinic school for a few years when I received what I have always taken to be a great honor. A group of graduate students in the Boston area with whom I had recently become friends, decided to pub-lish a compendium of information designed to guide a new generation of Jews back into Jewish practice. They called their anthology, THE JEWISH CATALOGUE. Not only was it a great idea, several hundred thousand Jews apparently thought so too because they bought the book. Two additional volumes of the catalogue were subse- quently brought out, creating a watershed in American Jewish publishing history. The JEWISH CATALOGUES be- came the principal guide-books for New Age Judaism, the Havurah movement, and the modest Jewish spiritual renewal which has blessed the final decades of this century.

In the back of the first CATALOGUE the editors cleverly decided to offer a list of "teachers" to whom prospective students might turn for further study. And, to my great delight and surprise, I was invited to offer my name along with a topic I felt competent to teach. Unfortunately, to my chagrin, the few topics I felt competent to teach were already being taught by some of the finest teachers in the world. Exasperated and properly chastened, I realized that, measured against such great scholars and rabbis, I had little if anything to teach. So, I returned the card &, in the space for "topic to teach," I wrote—as a joke—that I was fairly confident I at least could teach someone the most elementary imaginable topic, "the letters of the Hebrew alphabet."

That was the first joke. The second joke was that the editors apparently didn't think it was a joke and—

published my name as a teacher of the letters of the Hebrew alphabet. And, since readers of the CATA-LOGUE didn't know about either joke, I started getting calls and letters from around the country from prospective students who wanted to know what it. was I knew about the alphabet. They did not want to know how to read Hebrew, mind you, but about the mysteries of the letters. I began to do a little reading and that soon led to more serious research & finally the discovery of an elaborate, ancient, and mystical tradition. The end result was, of course, The Book of

LETTERS: A Mystical Alef-bait.

It is fitting that LETTERS and the JEWISH CAT-ALOGUE should be related, for the Book of LETTERS, like its more popular and important cousin, was also an early venture in the movement for American Jewish spiritual renewal. Unlike previous books about Jewish religious experience, the Mys-tical Alef-bait, was a book of spiritual encounter, a primary source. It was one of the first of a

New genre of books which would assume that the mystical dimension in Judaism was not confined to the past but a present possibility. And, like all, varieties of Jewish mysticism, it drew heavily on classical literary tradition. —

By evoking the layout of a page of Talmud with different blocks of text and opening from right to left or "backwards," LETTERS reached back into the tradition and sought to communicate graphically and physically with an emerging Jewishly literate readership. (Indeed, one reader reported buying a copy of LETTERS at half price from a bookseller who was convinced it was defectively bound.) I originally envisioned the book set in type but, because its layout was so unorthodox (or perhaps I should say, orthodox), I was compelled to provide elaborate sketches to help the publisher envision the finished product. My editor liked the sketches so much that she convinced me that the book would feel more authentic if it were literally a hand written manuscript. So I learned how to draw the letters.

Apparently, readers also have found LETTERS to be a learning experience. From correspondence and phone calls I've received over the years and from comments made to me when I teach in other communities, people report that LETTERS has served as a doorway for them to other dimensions of their own spiritual search. And they naturally have brought their own unique experiences to this process, discovering ways to use the book which I never dreamed of and which have in turn enhanced the book for me. I thought that other readers also might find their own search enriched and so, at the end of this new edition, I have added some of the primary ways others have used this book.

No reminiscence would be complete without reference to Marie Cantlon, my editor at Harper & Row, and her assistant, Cathy Nether, who tendered this book along the perilous road to publication. They were "the Heb-rew midwives," and I remain deeply grateful to them both. I am also honored that Stewart Matlins has chosen to reprint The Book of LETTERS as the first

13

title of his new press, Jewish Lights Publishing. He is a man of great spiritual vision and creative energy. There are very few publishers remaining in corporate America who still believe their primary job is simply to make important and beautiful books. Finally, I want to thank my wife, Haven, who continues to believe, despite much evidence to the contrary, that I am a religious man.

It has been fifteen years now since the first appearance of the BOOK of LETTERS. Since that time I have not learned any new ones. But I have learned of a tradition recounted in the thirteenth century Kabbalistic text, ספר התמונה, Sefer HaTemunah, that teaches that one letter is missing from our present Hebrew alphabet and that this letter will only be revealed in the future. The anonymous author goes on to explain that every defect in our present universe is mysteriously connected with this missing letter—an unimaginable consonant whose sound will create undreamed of words and worlds, transforming repression into loving.

14

You may have already noticed that on either side
of the black, leather tefillin box which is worn on
the forehead during morning prayers, are raised
letter shins. If you look closely, you will notice that
one of them, (the one on the left side) instead of
having three prongs, has four. It looks something
like this: Some suspect that this may be the
missing letter whose name & pronunciation must wait
for another universe. Yet nevertheless, every morning, we wear it right between our eyes!

LSK,
Eitz Rsah 5750
Sudbury, Massachusetts

introduction

Before you try to read this book there are a few things about the letters of the Hebrew alphabet or the אוֹתִיּוֹת OTiYOT it will help you to know.

The אוֹתִיּוֹת OTiYOT exist independently of ink and paper or even words. We learn that when Moses shattered the first set of tablets, the letters ascended to the One who gave them. And in another place, the story is told of Rabbi Hananya ben Teradyon that he was wrapped in a scroll of the Torah and burned at the stake. Moments before his death, his students cried out, "Master! What do you see?" He answered, "The parchment is burning, but the letters are flying toward the heavens!"

The אוֹתִיּוֹת OTiYOT have been around since before

16
יו

the creation of the world and are mysteriously linked with the creative process itself. It is told of the master builder of the wilderness tabernacle, Bezalel, that he knew how to combine the letters by which the heavens and the earth were made. And elsewhere we read that one of the last things Gd did before He rested on the seventh day from His world-work was to determine the precise shape of the letters.

The אותיות OTiYOT are more than just the signs for sounds. They are symbols whose shape & name, placement in the alphabet, & words they begin put them each at the center of a unique spiritual constellation. They are themselves holy. They are vessels carrying within the light of the Boundless One.

The אותיות OTiYOT have been sources of wisdom, meditation, and fantasy for the Jewish people all through their history. There have grown about each of them centuries-old traditions. One mystical alphabet after another. I hope with this book to keep that tradition alive for so many who have forgotten even some of the letters.

I have chosen a Hebrew alphabet adapted from the one used in Eastern European Torah scrolls, complete with the traditional scribal ornamentation. I think it is the holiest one. I have written the letters Bet ב Kaf כ Pey פ Shin ש and Tav ת with a dagesh or dot since they are most frequently named and pronounced as if the dagesh or the dot were present.

The transliterations are according to the way it seems to me that most people could most easily pronounce the word — except in cases where a traditional transliteration has become commonly accepted.

The commentary and additional legends are written vertically on each page and are drawn from Talmudic and Midrashic sources. The specific traditions describing the details of how to write each letter come from Mishnat Soferim which traditionally is printed in editions of Mishna Berura within the section dealing with the laws of Tefillin or phylacteries.

18
י״ח

After a while you will get to know each letter.
You will come to greet its shape and its sound like
an old friend. You will learn how to draw it and
how to use it and how to converse with it. It
will be open to you. And await your gaze.

בָּרוּךְ הַמְלַמֵּד אֶת יָדִי
לְסַפֵּר אֶת הָאוֹתִיּוֹת

Praised be He who has taught
my hand to scribe the letters.

Erev Purim 5735
24 February 1975
Sudbury, Massachusetts

Lawrence Kushner
יעקב בן אברהם קלונימוס

19
יט

Rabbi Elazar bar Abina said in Rabbi Aha's name: For 26 generations the Alef complained before G-d: I am the first of the letters yet You didn't create Your world with me! Don't worry, said G-d, the world and all its fulness were created for the Torah alone. Tomorrow when I come to give My Torah at Sinai the first word I say will begin with you.

Alef אֶלֶף is the first letter. It has no sound. Only the sound you make when you begin to make every sound. Open your mouth and begin to make a sound. STOP! That is Alef.

It is the letter beginning the first of G-d's mysterious 70 names: אֱלֹהִים ELOHIM. G-d. It also begins the most

important thing about Him:
אֶחָד ECHAD. One. Know that
G-d is One. The first and the last
and the only One.

The name of the first man was
אָדָם ADAM. Adam. The first
man. And the name of the her-
ald of the last man will be
אֵלִיָּהוּ ELIYAHU. Elijah.

The name of the first Jew is also.
Alef begun אַבְרָהָם AVRAHAM.
אָבִינוּ AHVEENU. Abraham, our father.

Alef is the letter of fire אֵשׁ AYSH.
A fire which flames but does not
destroy. That is how the Holy
One gets your attention. He shows
you the primordial fire.

The letter Alef א has in its upper right hand corner a mark which looks very much like the letter Yud ', and it is the custom of many scribes to place a small thorn or point on its top. This Yud is joined to the middle of the top of the body of the Alef.

And the very first letter of the first word of the first commandment begins with the first letter which has no sound: א Alef. אָנֹכִי ANOCHI. I.

"I am the Lord your G-d who brought you out of the land of Egypt, the house of slavery."

It is no accident that all these words begin with Alef. The most basic words there are begin with the most primal sound there is. The almost sound you make before you can make any sound.

The lower left hand mark of an Alef א also looks like the letter Yud ' suspended from the body of the א.

Bait ﬠ is drawn with two little points—one pointing above, the other pointing behind & toward the right. In this way when someone asks the Bait "Who made you?", it points above, and if they ask "What is His name?" it points toward the Alef, as if to say "One is His name."

The second letter, Bait בֵּית, is a house בַּיִת BAYIT. It is "of the ground. A house firmly set upon the earth. The dot which is called a dagesh represents one who lives within.

When Jacob our father slept in the wilderness, he was certain that he was alone. But when he awoke, he had learned about Bait: "Surely G-d has been in this place, and I didn't even know it!"

And so he named the place בֵּית אֵל BAIT AEL. A place of man became the house of G-d.

G-d has many houses בֵּית הַמִּקְדָּשׁ BAIT HA-MIKDASH. The ancient house of holiness. And בֵּית הַכְּנֶסֶת BAIT HA-KENESSET. The house of meeting and prayer. And בֵּית הַמִּדְרָשׁ BAIT HA-MIDRASH. The house of searching and study. They are all בֵּית Bait. The house of G-d.

All the other letters might fall over, but not a Bait. See how the base of a Bait is so close to the earth. The ground. Bend your knees to the ground and be blessed.

A blessing בְּרָכָה BERACHA.

Great care must be taken with the shape and the length of the Bait ב. For if it should appear more round than square, then it might be confused with a Kaf כ. Or if shorter than longer, then it might be confused with a Nun נ. And if there should be some doubt as to which of the two letters it is, then we ask a child to see if he can distinguish.

You can walk into a Bait, and you are at home. The Holy One wants us to be at home in His world. So the Torah begins with a Bait. בְּרֵאשִׁית BERESHEET. "In the beginning G-d created the heavens and the earth."

בראשית

Bait is the house G-d visits. The world is a home for those who remember who built the house.

For them it is filled with blessing, and it is a בַּיִת BAIT.

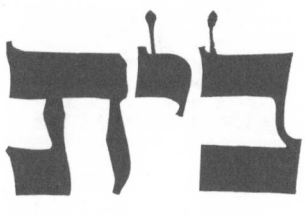

בית

Bait was chosen to commence the Torah to teach us that just as a Bait is closed on the top, the bottom, and the right side, but opens toward the left — in the direction of reading — so too should we concern ourselves with the day the world was created and onward. Here & now.

Gimmel גָּמַל is a wave rolling out into the world. Hear it: Gimmel. Gimmel. Gimmel.

Bait is the place of beginning. But Gimmel is the act of beginning. Eager to roll out and over itself in גִּלְגּוּל GIL-GOOL. Rolling.

There is a legend which tells that all the souls return again and again so that they might rise to ever higher rungs: one soul rolling throughout the generations גִּלְגּוּל נֶפֶשׁ. GIL-GOOL NEFESH. The transmigration of souls.

Wanting to do acts of loving-kindness גְּמִילוּת חֲסָדִים. GIMILUT HASIDIM,

Why is the foot of the Gimmel ג extended out to the left toward the Dalet ד, the next letter? Because it is befitting for the generous to run after the poor. And the Gimmel is generous and the Dalet is poor.

27
כז

deeds which are so generous, G-d does not even ask everyone to do them.

Yet, for each one of us there is a deed which cannot be asked which we must nevertheless offer. That is the only way. Striving to complete the work. גְמָרָא GEMARA. Completion.

That is the only reason to leave your house and go. And so Gimmel is great גָּדוֹל GADOL and mighty גִּבּוֹר GIBOR.

And one day all the souls doing acts of loving kindness גְּמִילוּת חֲסָדִים GIMILUT HASIDIM will rise into a great yearning wave that will reach to the heavens and fill the world with גְּאוּלָה GEULAH. Redemption.

גאולה

Care must be taken to insure that the foot of the Gimmel be joined to the stem but not so much that the tail is lost, lest it look like a Nun ן.

And why does the roof of the Dalet ד extend backwards a little to the right, in the direction of the Gimmel ג? To teach us that the poor man, Dalet, must make himself available to the Gimmel, the one who would lend him money. Nevertheless the Dalet is turned away—teaching that charity must be given in secret.

Dalet דלת is the door דלת DELET. Very few people know that they know about the Dalet. Even fewer open it, for they are afraid to go inside. Dalet is also the fourth letter.

And that is why there are four doors.

The first door is poor דַל DAHL. It is the nevertheless proud door of a poor man's home.

The second door was on our house long ago when we were slaves in Egypt. And on the night when the Lord, our G-d, brought us out from there with a mighty hand & an outstretched arm, our fathers slaughtered the Egyptian lamb-god and put the blood דָּם DAHM on the door דֶּלֶת DELET as a sign.

The Dalet ד should have a long roof and a short foot lest it be confused with the final Kaf ך whose foot goes below the line.

And so everyone would know which god we intended to serve.

There is another door. It opens the holy ark in which the scrolls of the Torah are kept. Above it is written: דַּע לִפְנֵי מִי אַתָּה עוֹמֵד DA LIFNEY MI ATA OMED

דע

Know before whom you stand. Know דַע DA. Know that when you stand before the Dalet, the door, you also stand before the Judge דַּיָּן DAYAHN. The One who sees into your heart. The One who judges the judges of flesh and blood.

The final door is binding your-self to G-d דְּבֵיקוּת D'VAY-KUT, so that He is never absent from your life. Never. Not even for a moment. There is only holiness. That is why doors are such mysterious things. Perhaps that is also why so many people are afraid to open the door of Dalet.

It is also important that the back of the Dalet's head – the upper right hand corner be clearly squared off, otherwise it might be confused with the Resh ר.

דְּבֵיקוּת

31

לא

The letter Hay ה is actually composed of two letters. Just there is a Dalet ד and then, in the lower left hand corner of the Dalet's space there is a Yud ׳. The Yud should be separate from the roof but not a greater distance than the thickness of the roof. The Yud leans toward the inside of the Dalet —otherwise it might make the Hay it look like the letter Tav ת.

Hay has almost a sound. The sound of breathing out. The most effortless noise a soul can make. And that's why there is some of Hay in every word. And also why Hay is so elusive for it is the sound of being present אֵ Hay. The letter of two letters facing one another.

Hay is the closest you can come to the Holy One, blessed be He. G-d says to each of us: אֶהְיֶה אֲשֶׁר אֶהְיֶה EHYEH ASHER EHYEH "I will be what I will be." Hay ה. Hey! I will be who I will be. Not who you want Me to be!

When two are married, they look at each other and whisper: Hay ה הֲרֵי אַתְּ מְקֻדֶּשֶׁת לִי HARAY AHT MIKU-DESHET LI. "Behold, I will try with all my being to be present for you." And

so the ה of הוּא HOO which means "He" and the ה of הִיא HEE which means "she" become the ה of הֵם HAYM which means "them".

It is essential that the two marks which make the Hay ה be discrete from each other. They must not touch or be connected to each other by even so much as a hair's breadth. If they do and even if a child can easily recognize it as what we may think is the letter Hay, it is nevertheless not the letter Hay.

G-d created two worlds: this one and the one to come. There is a tradition that He created this one with the letter Hay ה and the one to come with the letter Yod י. And why this world with the Hay? Because like this world it is easy to fall out the bottom. And also like this world there is always a tiny space just between the left leg and the roof so as always to permit another entrance. This is repentance.

While everyone can say, "I am present," only a very few can say הנני, "Here am I"; for to answer הנני means that you no longer belong only to yourself. To answer הנני means that you give the Hay ה of your being over to the One who calls. That is why Hay is the letter most often linked with G-d's name.

But there is still a greater Hay ה than "Behold." And this is the Hay ה of הנני HEENAYNI, "Here am I."

We read: "And you will eat And you will be sat-
isfied And you will enquire G-d." Real people And
real ideas And real actions are real because
they are separate, one from the other. Ever.

Such is not the way of real unity.
And then there would be only the one. But
would be dissolved into the "other,"
Otherwise the "one"
evident.
be joined because they are inde-
that "one" and "another" cannot
does not, precisely to remind us
another. But it
to join one and
like this: —. So as
joining should look
that the letter of
You would think
another.
of and. One and
And Vav is the sound
of being joined.
Vav וו is the sound

The head of the Vav I should not be longer than
it is thick lest it look like a Resh ר, and it
should be rounded on the upper right—hand
corner lest it be mistaken for the letter Zayin ז.

struggling to be unique. Since only one who is unique can be joined. And this is the work of Vav: to join us all into a myriad of constellations each remaining different, each bound to the other.

For this reason there can only be one word which begins with Vav. That is confession: וִדּוּי VI-DUI. Telling the sad truth where before there had only been a lie.

וידוי

And once you confess the sad truth, then, no matter what, you are joined to the one you told.

The Vav ו should have a long narrowing foot extending to the line. If it is too short it may be confused with the Yud '. And on the other hand, if it is too long it may be confused with a final Nun ן.

עוֹלָם יְמוֹת זְכֹר Z' CHOR Y'MOT OLAM, "Remember the days of the universe gone by."

Zayin זָכִין is masculine. זָכָר ZACHAR. And there he remembers זָכַאֶר ZACHAER, everything.

And belongs to this man a beard זָקָן ZAKAN. And this man is old זָקֵין ZAKAYN. And this man can look back through time זְמַן Z'MAN, and he remembers זָכָר ZACHAER, everything.

Raba said (speaking of the letters of the Torah scroll, Tefillin and Mezzuzot) that there are seven letters which require three strokes or "tagin" on their tops. Each of the strokes resembles a tiny Zayin ז.

The seven letters which may be adorned with "tagin" or little crowns are: שַׁעַטְנֵז גֵּץ or the SHAT-NAYZ GAYTZ letters. Shin. Ayin. Tet. Num. Zayin. Gimmel and Tsadi. Each one contains the letter Zayin.

זֵכֶר צַדִּיק לִבְרָכָה ZACHAER TSADIK LIV-RACHA. "The memory of a righteous one is a blessing." זֵכֶר עֲמָלֵק ZACHAER AMALEK. "Remembering what the wicked have done." זֵכֶר לִיצִיאַת מִצְרַיִם ZACHAER LI'TZI-AT MITZ-RAYIIM. "Remember how G-d brought us out of Egypt." זָכוֹר אֶת יוֹם הַשַּׁבָּת ZACHOR ET YOM HA-SHABBAT. "Remember the Shabbat."

And because with Zayin there is memory, there is also a light which shines from one end of the universe to the other. Zohar זֹהַר ZOHAR. The Book of Light, the volumes of splendor.

Many believe the light has been forever lost. But this is not so. It is only because we ignore the sacred vessel of Light: memory.

And Zayin is the seed זֶרַע ZERA. The seed a man remembers to plant for the future. Remember, you are a seed which has been sown for yet another future.

If the foot of the Zayin's is too long, extending below the line, then it will be confused with a final Nun f. If, on the other hand, its head is not clearly squared off, then it will be confused with the Vav !.

38
חל

The Chet חית of the Torah scroll, tefillin and mezzuzot is composed of two Zayins ז whose roofs are joined with a hunch at the center forming a steep roof.

In the Torah the Chet חי״ת is written with a sharp jagged notch on its forehead. It is almost as if there were two separate letters barely joined together.

They need each other to stand. But they wish they did not. So they barely touch.

Chet is the agony of a soul torn apart from itself. The top of your throat and the bottom of your throat fighting against one another

39
חט

Create the sound of the Chet. This is the reason why the chet yields so many strange and conflicted word pairs:

Sin is חטא CHAIT. A soul torn against itself because it is sure that it is pious.

While a חסיד CHASID, a pious one, is a soul convinced that it commits many sins.

Pang is חבל CHAVEL. Almost dying from birthwork. Bringing forth life.

While life is חיים CHAYIM. Almost dying and almost living from bringing forth life.

Desecration is חלול CHILUL. The secularization which knows no sanctity and can only drive souls apart.

While a little group is a חבורה CHAVURAH. A small society of souls who join together to accomplish some holy task.

Destruction is חורבן CHURBAN. Devastation which always seems to be the end.

While the marriage canopy is חפה CHUPPA. A shelter protecting the seedling of another generation.

40
מ

It is the custom of some scribes to put one crownlet or tag just above the top of the left foot.

And this is why at the end of a book of the Torah and at the beginning of something difficult we say חזק CHAZAK, Be strong!

חזק

Learn from what has gone before that strength is not of might and force but of endurance and balance.

The letter Tet ט has two heads. The left head and leg have the appearance of the letter Zayin ז and are adorned with three crownlets or tagin.

You cannot pronounce the letter Tet טית until you go out early in the spring morning and see the dew טל TAL.

Only when you secretly confess to yourself that you really do not understand how the tiny droplets of water have come to be, are you permitted to be cleansed in them. And wrap yourself in your prayer shawl טלית TALIT.

By what miracle is there dew? And why is there grass? And why are there dew and rain וּמָטָר לְ _ TAL U'MATAR, the water sustaining life!

And by what blessing am I given life?

And so you dip yourself טְבִילָה T'VELAH. And wash yourself of the defilement טֻמְאָה TUM-AH which encrusts a soul. Then you will again find purity טָהֳרָה TAHARA. For Tet is pure and good.

"And G-d saw all that He had made and behold it was good טוֹב TOV."

Tet is good טוֹב TOV. It is good to be alive. Good to give thanks to the Lord. טוֹב לְהוֹדוֹת TOV L'HO-DOT.

Yud י"וד is the smallest letter. The easiest letter to draw. All you need to do is to touch your pen to the paper and you have drawn a Yud. It is so tiny that some-times people even forget to put it into words they are spelling. So what does the Yud do? It appears in another word.

G‑d is like that too. Thus the Yud most often represents His Name. And the Jewish people also claim it for their own. Like a dove יוֹנָה YONA soaring beyond the

There is a tradition which tells that the world to come was created with the letter Yud, for just as it is bowed down so will it be with the arrogant in the future.

heavens. A dove searching anxiously for a place to alight: G-d, the Jewish people, & the smallest letter.

Something of the Yud participates in the upper worlds. This is the Yud of יְרוּשָׁלַיִם YERUSHALAYIM the heavenly city of G-d. Something of the Yud breathes of the lower worlds. This is the Yud of יֵצֶר YETZER. The inclination of a person toward evil.

So it is that the Yud flies between them both so that there can be unification יִחוּד YICHUD, a joining of the upper and the lower worlds.

Yud is the hand of G-d יַד חֲזָקָה YAD CHAZAKA, a strong hand bringing us out of slavery. Yud is the hand a person uses so that he will not lose his place in the Torah: 7, Yad. A hand. Yud is the tenth letter. A person has ten fingers.

Yud is all that remained of Jacob יַעֲקֹב YAKOV our father after he wrestled with G-d and men to become Israel יִשְׂרָאֵל YISRA-EL. A "pintele Yid". A tiny Jew within each and every Jew and no bigger than a Yud.

The letter Kaf ⊃ can easily be confused with two letters. If its upper or lower right corners are more square than round, it will look like a Bait ⊐. If, on the other hand, its base and its roof are too short then it will look like the letter Nun ⌐.

Kaf כַּף is the palm of a hand כַּף KAF filled with sincerity כַּוָּנָה KAVANAH.

Kaf is a cup כּוֹס KOS filled with blessing both for those who hold it and for those who drink from it.

It contains all the honor a child can bestow on his mother & father. כִּבּוּד אָב וָאֵם KIBBUD AHV VA-AIM, Honor of mother and father. That is all there is. כָּל KhOL, All.

To take your parents seriously is the hardest commandment. To offer them the cup without spilling it. To receive from them the cup without gulping. Such is Kaf. The cup of blessing. A goblet of honor. A crown כֶּתֶר KETER for your head.

But only he shall drink who has himself spilled and gulped and wept.

Only he who has learned that not all intentions are as they seem.

Only he who is beaten כָּתִית KATEET, like oil which has been beaten from olives, until he is כָּשֵׁר KASHER, pure and fit, shall drink.

Then Kaf transforms itself into the crown.

But of course once you have reached the rung of "The Crown" כֶּתֶר KETER you

47
מז

Care must be taken to extend the final half ך below the line so that it will not be confused with the letters Resh ר or Dalet ד.

There are five letters which have a different form when they appear at the end of a word: Kaf כך, Mem מם, Nun נן, Pey פף, and Tsadi צץ.

would sooner give the crown to your mother and father. Never forget that your parents were the instruments Gd used to bring you into the world, and so must then be the instruments through whom you shall return to Him.

Lammed לָמֶד Oh so beautiful Lammed. Tall and elegant like a palm branch לוּלָב LULAV waved high.

Lammed is a student. At night לַיְלָה LILAH, by the moon לְבָנָה L'VANAH. forever לְעוֹלָם L'OLAM, while everyone else is asleep. Lammed studies the holy books.

Yet while its body may be curled in the midst of the study place, its heart לֵב LAEV soars like a flame: לַהַב LAHAV above all the other letters. From the wisdom

Rabbi Yose likened the Lammed ל to a town watchman who stands on a high lookout and calls out his warning.

49
מט

The Lammed ל is actually composed of two separate letters. It is the Vav ו perched on the roof of the letter Kaf.

To see ahead comes the strength to say no. "Thou shalt not," לֹא LO. An idol says yea. Always yea. But one who studies the words of the Living God also hears "Thou shalt not." So the Lammed was chosen to say no.

Come my beloved, לְכָה דוֹדִי LECHA DODI Lammed. Teach me. Study with me. Tell me of the thirty-six righteous ones לָמֶד וָו צַדִּיקִים LAMMED VAV TSADIKIM who carry in their hearts the pain of all the world.

If you understand how bread לֶחֶם LECHEM and flame לַהַב LAHAV and to learn לִלְמֹד LILMOD and heart לֵב LEV all share in Lammed, then perhaps you are also a Lammed.

The Mem ם also is the result of the combination of two separate letters, the Kaf כ and the Vav ו. The Vav is attached at the back of its neck by one point to the forehead of the Kaf.

Mem מ is the substance of mother earth. It is water מַיִם MAYIM and it is the wilderness מִדְבָּר MIDBAR through which we wander and are made ready.

It is the food מַאֲכָל MA-ACHAL and the work מְלָאכָה M'LA-CHA which we must do for food.

And it is the work we must not do in order to rest מִנְחָה MINUCHA and keep the Shabbat.

That is why Mem is the שַׁמָּשׁ MAMASH, the stuff by which life in this world is sustained: Food מַאֲכָל MA-ACHAL. Water מַיִם MAYIM. Wilderness מִדְבָּר MIDBAR. Work מְלָאכָה M'LA-CHA. And מִצְוֹות MITZVOT.

And Mitzvot. Holy commandments. Given to us by the Holy One through Moses, our teacher: מֹשֶׁה רַבֵּינוּ MOSHE RABEYNU. Covenant obligations.

Sacred laws like the lights of a מְנוֹרָה MENORAH which transform the ordinary candlestick of everyday into the ecstasy of cleaving to G-d.

Mark it upon your doorposts מְזוּזוֹת MEZZUZOT. Lest you forget why you

Since the final Mem ם and the Samech ס are so similar, great care must be taken to insure that the final Mem has easily recognizable corners on the bottom while the letter Samech, on the other hand, be rounded.

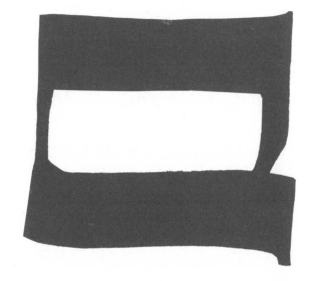

One tradition teaches that the ten utterances were written on the original tablets of stone in such a way that each letter went clear through to the other side. Rabbi Hisda taught that the letters final Mem and Samech ם ס, which each enclose a space, nevertheless, remained intact by what we can only assume was a miracle.

This then is the Mem's chariot מֶרְכָּבָה MERKABAH, Ascending unto the redeemer מָשִׁיחַ MASHIACH, Himself.

work, Lest you forget for Whom you work.

The Nun ‏נ‏ has the head of a Zayin ‏ז‏; its neck descends from the middle of the bottom of the head getting gradually thicker and leaning back slightly to the right. Cave must be taken not to make the Nun too long, otherwise it might easily be confused with the Bait ‏ב‏.

Nun ‏[נ]‏ is a soulbird ‏נְשָׁמָה‏ N'SHAMA. She is easily frightened and falls away silent. Just like a person ‏נֶפֶשׁ‏ NEFESH. In each person and in each soulbird there is something feminine ‏נְקֵבָה‏ N'KAYVA.

Ecstatic with a melody ‏נִגּוּן‏ NIGGUN. Melody on top of melody on top of melody. Going higher and lower at the same time. Dizzy and frightened yet unable to return.

54
‏נד‏

The final Nun must extend well below the line lest it look like the Vav.

Before and after Numbers 10:35-36 there are two upside down Nuns. No one knows why.

Nun is what is holy in a person. Faithful נֶאֱמָנָה NEH-EMANAH even unto the end. Like the tiny eternal light נֵר תָּמִיד NER TAMID, burning in a temple through the nights of its disbelief. So there shines a spark נִיצוֹץ NITZOTZ in each one of us. Some burn brighter. Some flicker. A light that can never be extinguished, only sealed off by wicked deeds.

And then when you die, the Nun, the soulbird returns to G-d who warms her and blesses her and sends her out again.

Hurling herself through laughter and tears, cascading waterfalls of wonders נִפְלָאוֹת NIFLA-OT. You do not open your eyes to see Nun, you close them.

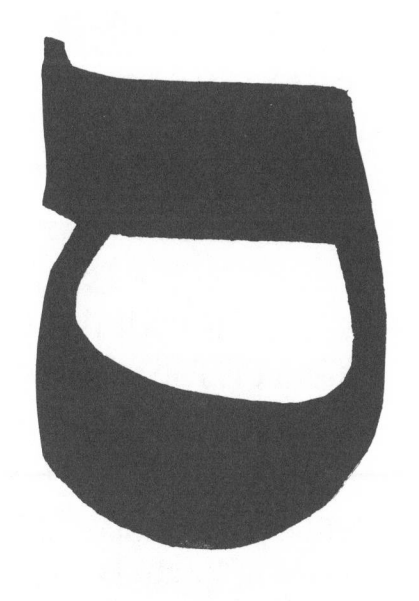

The roof of the letter Samech ס should be long and level; the base should be rounded, so as not to confuse it with the final Mem ם and there are many scribes who write it so that it touches the base line at only one point.

Samech סָמֶךְ is dwelling in the סֻכָּה SUKKA. A flimsy harvest hut. The letter which completely encloses a space within itself. It is the quiet sure smile one has when finding a shelter.

When you have been wandering for a long time and you come upon the mountain called סִינַי SINAI, this too is the shelter of Samech.

56
נג

The upper left-hand corner of the samech ס should, unlike the other three corners, be squared and extend over equal to the length of the letter Vav.

But why must all the shelters of Samech appear so transient? Only to teach you that G-d's shelter is unlike man's. Only He who gave you life can keep you in life. For one who knows this there is no anxiety. The Samech is all around him.

And just this is the shelter of the Holy One: Knowing the order of His prayers סִדוּר SIDDUR. And His meals סֵדֶר SEDER. And His books סֵפֶר SEFER and His Torah סֵפֶר תּוֹרָה SEFER TORAH.

When you discover why one tiny letter follows another, when you see through another layer of their inner meaning to a deeper secret סוֹד SOD, when you are so happy you are beyond joy, you are in the Samech.

This is the meaning of to lean: סוֹמֵך SO-MAYCH on His order. Each matter leans upon the next, and the sheltering presence is all around you.

57

The Ayin ע begins with a Yud "whose tail is first extended down and then on an angle toward the left. It gradually thickens and continues on below the base line. To the left of the Yud we draw a Zayin ז with a very narrow body which is then connected to the extension on the Yud.

Ayin ע does not speak. It only sees. It is an eye. עַ AYIN. Close your eyes. Open your mouth. Now try to see. That is the sound of Ayin.

It is the silent humility עֲנָוָה ANAVAH of serving the Master of the Universe. Serving. Worshiping עֲבוֹדָה AVODAH. Emptying yourself so that you can be filled with G-d.

But not all who serve, serve the living G-d. To Ayin also belongs the Ayin of the golden calf עֵגֶל AGEL and the Ayin of the perverse service of a fetish, of an idol: עֲבוֹדָה זָרָה AVODAH ZARA. This is the Ayin of slavery which shames. עֲבָדִים הָיִינוּ AVADIM HA-YINU. "We were slaves..."

But there is also an Ayin of service which frees. The great collar, the yoke עֹל OHL by which the ox serves his master is not his shame but his fulfillment. This is the purpose for which

It is important that the two heads of Ayin y not touch one another. This perhaps is because the Ayin is a joining of two letters: the Yod' and the Zayin ?

(In the same way that other letters result from the combination of 2 and 3 letters) and their respective discreteness must be preserved.

you were set on this earth: to serve G-d. To take upon yourself the yoke of the kingdom of Heaven.

This is why the Ten Commandments, the ten utterances עֲשֶׂרֶת הַדִּבְּרֹות ASERET HA-DIBROTE which tell us how to begin to serve are Ayin begun. And the holy books which tell how our fathers have served are also Ayin חַיִּם עֵץ AYTZ CHAYIM. They are a tree of life.

Rabbi Akiba taught that every stroke in the Torah, even the tiny crownlets or tagin over the letters תָּגִיּן, is a vehicle for teaching us about G-d.

עֵץ חַיִּים

"It is a tree of life for those who hold on to it."

60

The letter Pey פ is drawn a little larger than other letters in order that it can curl into itself without touching, and if it does, it becomes invalid.

Ayin may be an eye which has no mouth. But Pey פֵא is a mouth which has no eyes. Mouth. פֶּה PEH.

At first because Pey has no eyes, everything seems simple פְּשָׁט P'SHAT. Whatever your mouth first says without looking beyond.

But nothing is simple. Just as everything conceals a myriad of layers and contradictions and meanings, so it is with PEY. The dagesh-dot inside is someone who has already entered any labyrinth. One who searches.

"Open the gates" פִּתְחוּ שְׁעָרִים PIT-CHU SH'ARIM. Let my mouth be open. Not to see what first meets my eye. Let my mouth be open so that it can proclaim the awe and intricacy of each occurrence. For everything is a miracle פֶּלֶא PELEH. Everything is a vehicle and everyone is a messenger.

Know that there is an orchard

It happened once that the teachers didn't come to the house of study. The children who were there said: Let us study the letters without them. Why do the letters פ ך צ ץ כ ן ם have final forms? To teach us that the Torah was transmitted: מֵאֹמֶר Ma-amar saying by saying. Nun נֶאֱמָן Neh-eman the faithful to the faithful; Tsadi צַדִיק Tsadik the righteous to the righteous; Pey פֶּה Peh mouth to mouth, and Kaf כַּף Kaf from hand to hand.

62
10

פַּרְדֵּ**ﭖ** PARDES. Its corners **ﭖ**אוֹת PAYOT
belong to the poor and its fruit **ﭖ**רִי P'REE
is the wisdom of all which is hidden. The
beauty of all
which is concealed.

For every simple
ﭖשַׁט PESHAT
word in the Torah
there are hints
and stories and
secrets and
allusions which
summon us
into their intri-
cate mysteries.

The path into
the Pey-mouth
spirals back
into itself. So
it goes with this
eyeless mouth.

Care must be taken with the part of the final Pey ף which is curled under, that it not extend outward to the left otherwise it might be confused with the letter Tav ת.

The letter Tsadi צ is composed of a Nun נ whose head leans forward and whose neck, as a consequence, is stretched out and whose foot is extended so as to provide balance like this: נ. A Yud is then attached by its tail to the middle of the back of the Nun's neck.

Tsadi 'צדי is the first letter in time. While other letters are first in the Alef-Bait or in grace or even in importance, the first letter the Holy One formed was Tsadi. For Tsadi is righteousness and "Deeds of Giving are the very foundation of the world". צֶדֶק TSEDEK, righteousness.

To make room for the other letters, the Lord of Hosts had to step back & remove Himself—in the way a father must restrain himself so that his little child will have room to grow. This is צִמְצוּם TSIMTSUM self-withdrawal. making yourself small so that another can grow.

Even so that you too can grow. Deeds of giving: deeds of making yourself less: deeds of making another more: such deeds are צְדָקָה TS'DAKA. And one who does them, a righteous one, a צַדִיק TSADIK. "The righteous shall inherit the earth."

There is a legend which teaches that when Moses got to the top of Mt. Sinai to receive the Torah, he found G-d putting on the finishing touches, the Tagin-crownlets. What are those? asked Moses. Never mind, answered G-d. You will be more than busy enough trying to understand the meaning of the letters themselves without worrying about such things. Someday a yet unborn student will discover their meaning.

No one can be a Tsadik alone. There must be at least nine others. We are able to rise to the rung of Ts'daka only by binding ourselves with others who also could never make it alone. This then is a congregation צִבּוּר TSIBUR. Ts'daka, deeds of giving, are the reason for a congregation.

And this then is the reason that Tsadi is the very foundation of the earth. The rock צוּר TSUR. The goal צִיּוֹן TSIYON. And the mysterious fringes צִיצִת TSITSIT which ever remind us of the commandments, our rock and our goal. "Make for yourselves fringes on the corners of your garments."

Rabbi Eliezer taught that the five letters which have final forms: כ"ם נ"ף צ"ץ carry with them the "secret of redemption" by which the night of redemption was known beforehand to our fathers.

66
10

The bottom of the Kof קוף is a man calling "Holy" so that he can join himself to his Creator. The top line, sheltering & reaching down, is the Holy One.

Kof is the voice of an angel calling קָדוֹשׁ קָדוֹשׁ קָדוֹשׁ KADOSH KADOSH KADOSH "Holy holy holy is the Lord of Hosts."

Why is the single crownlet on the roof of the Kof ק turned toward the wicked Resh ר —the next letter? Because the Holy One says that if the wicked repents, I will set upon his head a crown as beautiful as the one on My head.

Kof is the voice קוֹל KOL of a person proclaiming the oneness of G-d

קְרִיאַת שְׁמַע K'RI-AT SHEMA. And the holiness of G-d קַדִּישׁ KADDISH. And the holiness of a Shabbat or of a festival קִדּוּשׁ KIDDUSH. And the holiness of a spouse קִדּוּשִׁין KIDDUSHIN. Kof is the voice of holiness.

Nothing can be holy without the voice of Kof to say it is. But remember also that with your voice you can make the whole world holy קָדוֹשׁ KADOSH.

Kof is one of the letters made by two marks. Hay ה is the other. The lower mark of the Kof is man calling G-d. But G-d also calls man! With the upper mark of the Kof He whispers very softly

The roof of the Kof ק should be level and have a tiny crownlet leaning forward. The roof itself looks very much like the letter Kaf's כ except that its base is shorter than the Kaf's and curls just a little bit.

to see if you are really listening: קוֹל דְּמָמָה דַקָּה KOL D'MAMA DAKA. a voice which is still and small. A little girl. The daughter of a voice, G‑d's voice בַּת קוֹל BAT KOL. Like an echo. Always listen.

Such is Kof. The voice by which man allows G‑d to be present by calling: Holy קָדוֹשׁ KADOSH. And the voice by which G‑d asks if man wants Him to be.

"Holy, holy, holy is the Lord of Hosts. The fulness of the whole earth is His glory."

The foot of the letter Kof ק should be aligned directly under the left-most point of its roof. Care should be taken so that the foot at no point intersects the roof.

The Resh ר must be drawn with great care. If the corner at the back of its head is not clearly rounded, it will look like a Dalet ד. If its roof is too short, it will look like a Vav ו, and if its tail is too long, it will look like a final Kaf ך.

Resh רֵישׁ is the יֵצֶר הָרָע YETZER HA-RA. The inescapable wish to believe that you are closer to G-d than anyone else.

That is why Resh goes up and down in the land as a gossip רָכִיל RACHIL. A tale bearer. And commits the gravest sin לְשׁוֹן הָרָע L'SHON HA-RA. The evil tongue. So arrogant that it

70
ע

believes that it can speak about someone else.

Look. When the Yud ׳ which is a Jew makes himself big and proud, he becomes the Resh ר. Wicked רָשָׁע RASHA. This is the Resh which pretends not to know that it is evil.

There is another kind of Resh. This is the end of pretending. רֹאשׁ הַשָּׁנָה ROSH HASHANA, the day of admitting. Master of the Universe! רִבּוֹנוֹ שֶׁל עוֹלָם RIBONO SHEL OLAM, have compassion רַחֲמִים RACHAMIM on your children. The harder a soul tries, the harder yet it must try. And this is the striving of Resh. That one who is pious knows he is far closer to wickedness than someone who is in between. This is how he became pious.

Look. With so little as a smudge, the Dalet ד of אֶחָד ECHAD G-d is "One" becomes the Resh ר of אַחֵר ACHAER "another." And the world is destroyed.

71

עא

Something of Shin שׁן is shattering. The breaking of the primeval vessels שְׁבִירַת הַכֵּלִים SH'VI-RAT HA-KALIM. The discord and confusion which is the beginning of growing. And then trying to get it all back together again.

Sound the great ram's horn. Sound the שׁוֹפָר SHOFAR. Bring home from exile all those who have been banished. Gather together all the broken pieces.

Shin is the letter just before the end. It is the fitting together of all the parts. The restoration of all the scattered shards. This is Shin: Peace שָׁלוֹם SHALOM. Completion. Wholeness.

So at last there is rest. The seventh day שַׁבָּת SHABBAT. The suspension of anxiety. Shin is the keeper of Shabbat שׁוֹמֵר שַׁבָּת SHOMER SHABBAT. A mother lights the Shabbat lights and gathers in the שֶׁפַע SHEFA resplendent radiance of Shin into her home. And the presence of the Holy One is among us: שְׁכִינָה SHECHINA.

On the doorpost of every Jewish home there is a Shin. This is the Shin of שַׁדַּי SHADDAI G-d's most mysterious name. It is also the Shin of שִׂים שָׁלוֹם SIM SHALOM. Let G-d be present in this home. "Let there be peace."

It is important that each of shin's שׁ three heads not intersect, and some put a crown on the center Yud.

The Tav ת begins with a ר to which we add its left foot. It begins in the middle of the underside of the roof. The left foot should stop directly under the end of the roof. The right foot should not be too long lest an average child confuse it with the final Peh ך.

Tav ות is the mark ות TAV that Gd writes on the parchment of man. It is the letter which they both have in common. And since this need to share is the reason for all the letters, it is the last letter.

Tav is the sound of Gd and the sound of man. This is the most precious sound; it is the most beloved. Together, Gd and man have formed the Tav.

Tav is the name of man calling Gd תְּפִילָה TEFILA. Prayer. Tav is the name of man singing Gd's praises תְּהִלִים TEHILIM. Psalms. Tav is the sound of man returning to Gd תְּשׁוּבָה TESHUVA. Returning. Tav is the mysterious small black boxes תְּפִילִין TEFILIN. The phylacteries we bind on our arms and on our foreheads during prayer & study.

And Tav is the sound of Gd speaking to man תּוֹרָה TORAH. It is the marking down of what our people hear Gd saying. So it is the first five books: סֵפֶר תּוֹרָה SEFER TORAH. And the twenty-four books of the Bible: תַּנַ"ךְ TANACH. And

One legend tells that Gd told Gavriel to put a mark, a Tav, on the foreheads of the righteous and a mark, a Tav, of blood on the foreheads of the wicked. And in another place Rab said that Tav begins תִּחְיֶה TICH-YEH "You shall live" and תָּמוֹת TA-MOOT "You shall die". Tav is both of them.

the sixty-three tractates of the
תַּלְמוּד TALMUD. And the total of all
the six hundred thirteen commandments
תַּרְיַ"ג TARYAG. Six hundred thirteen.

Tav proves that it is possible for
a letter to capture something between
man and G-d. And the commandment
which ensues.

This is why Tav is also תִּקֻּן TIKKUN.
Mending. The repairing of the universe. In truth אֱמֶת EMET indeed.
The last letter. For Tav is the letter
and the task of G-d and man.

Resh Lakish said that the Tav תּ is the
last letter of the Holy One's seal, for Rav Hanina
taught that the seal of G-d is אֱמֶת EMET, truth.

תם ונשלם

complete & concluded

76
עו

Ways readers have used the Book of LETTERS:

א An introduction to learning Hebrew.

ב A meditation guide.

ד Reflecting on the letters of one's Hebrew name.

ז A primer for beginning students of Hebrew calligraphy.

ה Studying the letters as rubrics of Jewish spirituality.

for children

Because Nothing Looks Like God
     (with Karen Kushner)
The Book of Miracles: A Young Person's Guide
     to Jewish Spiritual Awareness
How Does God Make Things Happen?
     (with Karen Kushner)
     SkyLight Paths Publishing Board Book
In God's Hands
     (with Gary Schmidt)
What Does God Look Like?
     (with Karen Kushner)
     SkyLight Paths Publishing Board Book
Where Is God?
     (with Karen Kushner)
     Sky Light Paths Publishing Board Book

Fiction

Kabbalah: A Love Story
     Morgan Road Books

"Open Other End"

All you need to know is English to read these pages, but the format of this book is Hebrew—opening from right to Left. This is the end of the book, not the beginning.

Other books by Lawrence Kushner

The Book of WORDS: Talking Spiritual Life, Living Spiritual Talk

Eyes Remade for WONDER: A Lawrence Kushner Reader

Filling WORDS with LIGHT: Hasidic & Mystical Reflections on Jewish Prayer (with Nehemiah Polen)

GOD Was in this PLACE & I, i Did not Know: Finding Self, Spirituality and Ultimate Meaning

Honey from the Rock: An Introduction to Jewish Mysticism

I'm God; You're Not: Observations on Organized Religion & Other Disguises of the Ego

Invisible Lines of Connection: Sacred Stories of the Ordinary

Jewish Spirituality: A Brief Introduction for Christians

The River of Light: Jewish Mystical Awareness

The Way into Jewish Mystical Tradition

see over for books for children & fiction